All THINGS COWS For Kids

FILLED WITH PLENTY OF FACTS, PHOTOS, AND FUN TO LEARN ALL ABOUT COWS

ANIMAL READS

WWW.ANIMALREADS.COM

THIS BOOK BELONGS TO...

_____

_____

WWW.ANIMALREADS.COM

THE MOO ROUTE!

Welcome to the Wonderful World of Cows!......1

Who's Who in the Moo Crew? 5

Built for the Moo Life: 15
    What Makes a Cow a Cow

Munch & Crunch: 29
    What Cows Love to Eat

The Moo-niverse of Cows: 37
    Meet the Breeds

Where in the World Do Cows Live? 57

Growing Up Bovine: 65
    From Wobbly Calf to Mighty Cow

Mind-Blowing Mooing Facts! 71

Congratulations— 77
    You're Now a Certified Cattle Whisperer!

Thank You! 81

WELCOME TO THE WONDERFUL WORLD OF COWS!

Cows might seem ordinary because we see them so often—but don't be fooled. These gentle giants are extraordinary and some of the most fascinating animals on Earth.

Think about it: they can take plain old grass (*which humans can't even digest!*) and turn it into milk. That milk becomes cheese, yogurt, and even ice cream. **Now *that's* a real-life superpower!**

And the surprises don't stop there. Did you know that a cow's heart is about the size of a basketball? Or that they can smell things from six miles away? That's like sniffing a snack from the other side of town! Also, even though they may look calm and slow, an enthusiastic cow can run 25 miles an hour. That's faster than most people on their best day!

Cows can swim, remember faces for years, and even have best friends they love to spend time with.

And those moos?

They're not all the same. Each one sounds a little different—as if cows use special names for one another.

Some cows have wild horns longer than you are tall, and others have fluffy coats that make them look like walking teddy bears. Cows have helped humans in all sorts of ways, and in some places, they're even treated like royalty.

ALL THINGS COWS FOR KIDS 3

In this book, you'll meet cows from around the world, peek inside their amazing bellies, and find out how calves grow up into mighty moo-machines.

So let's head into the pasture and meet them properly, shall we?

Get ready for an **UDDERLY** *amazing adventure.*

We promise you will never look at a cow the same way again.

WHAT IS A COW'S FAVORITE NEWSPAPER?

The Daily Moos

WHO'S WHO IN THE MOO CREW?

Ever heard someone say, "That's *not a cow, that's a bull!*" and wondered what they were talking about? Let's break it down so you'll always know who's who in the herd.

When we see **cattle** (*that's the word for a whole group*), most people will simply call them all "cows." But not every animal out there is actually a cow. A *cow* is a grown-up female that has had a baby. A *bull* is a grown-up male instead. You can usually tell them apart by their size—males are usually bigger and more muscular than females.

Think of cattle like a big family. The girls are cows, the boys are bulls, and the babies are called *calves*. A young male calf that's growing up but not a bull yet is called a ***bullock***—kind of like a teenager! And young girls who haven't had babies yet are called ***heifers*** (you say it like HEF-ers).

We might not be used to these names, but farmers use them to tell the animals apart and to help keep track of who's who on their farm.

A SPECIAL KIND OF ANIMAL

Cows belong to a group of animals called *mammals*. That might sound like a new *sciencey* word, but you already know lots of mammals—like dogs, cats, elephants... even humans!

Mammals all share a few key traits:

1. They have hair or fur (yep, cows have fur, even though it is usually short!)

2. They drink milk from their mothers when they're babies.
3. They're warm-blooded, meaning their bodies stay warm even when it's cold outside.
4. Mammals also give birth to live babies instead of laying eggs like fish and reptiles.

And there's one more thing that makes mammals extra special: babies really rely on their moms for food and protection at first. Cow mothers are gentle and protective, always keeping an eye on their

Hold up—you, reading this right now, are a mammal just like me?!

calves to make sure they're well-fed and safe. For the first few months, calves stay close to their mothers, learning how to be a cow while growing stronger and braver every day.

Zoologists—*those are animal scientists*—love sorting animals into groups. It's kind of like how you might organize your toys: stuffed animals in one box, building blocks in another, art stuff in a third. It helps make sense of the wild and wonderful animal world.

I'm a mountain goat—part of the Bovidae family, just like cows! You could say I'm a distant cousin.

Cows belong to a big group called the **Bovidae family**—a ginormous group of animals that are all related to one another. *And guess what?* The cow's cousins are buffalo, bison, goats, sheep, and even antelopes. They might not all look like cows, but they share some cool features—like hooves that are split in two and a super-special stomach system that helps them chow down on tough plants.

Now, if we zoom in a little closer, we learn that most cows we see on farms belong to a group called

Bos taurus. There is another branch of the family tree called *Bos indicus*. These are cows that live in hot places in parts of Asia and Africa, and they have a unique hump on their backs to help them handle the heat. Same family, some similarities, but also unique—like cousins!

See this hump? It helps me keep cool in hot places!

COWS: THE TAMED WILD THINGS

Here's a bit of wild history: today's cows are related to giant wild oxen called **aurochs** (say it like "OR-ocks"). These giants once roamed across Europe, Asia, and northern Africa thousands of years ago. They were tough, powerful, and much bigger than the cows we see today—more like something out of a legend than a peaceful farm animal.

This is a Heck cattle. It looks a lot like what an aurochs looked like long ago!

The last aurochs vanished in 1627, deep in a forest in Poland. But people had been working with them long before that. About 10,000 years ago, early farmers began choosing the calmest, most useful aurochs to raise. Over many generations, those wild, powerful animals slowly became the gentle, grass-chomping cows we know today.

Just like you might have your dad's smile or your grandma's curly hair, cows also carry traits from their wild ancestors. They've kept their strong legs for standing all day and their amazing ability to turn plain grass into energy (*don't worry—we'll explain how that works soon!*).

These days, cows are much more chilled out. They spend most of their days munching grass, snoozing under shady trees, and curiously watching the world go by. If you've ever had a cow wander over and stare at you through a fence, don't take it as bad manners—it's just cow curiosity. Cows are so curious that scientists have seen them taking turns to inspect new objects—like a herd of slow, mooing detectives! So when they walk over to check you out, they simply want to know what you're up to!

Hi! Hello! Howdy! Hey! Yo!

BUILT FOR THE MOO LIFE:
WHAT MAKES A COW A COW

Ever really looked at a cow and thought, "Why do they look like *that*?" Those big eyes... the swishy tail... the strong hooves—it's not just random. Every part of a cow's body helps it do cow things, whether that's munching grass, keeping cool, or staying steady on muddy ground.

So let's take a closer look at what makes a cow a cow—from head to tail—and find out why they're built just right for the farm life (*and maybe a little fence-staring, too*).

HORNS: NATURE'S HEADGEAR

Some cattle sport impressive horns growing right from their heads, while others don't have any horns at all. But those horns aren't just for looks—they're built for some serious business.

Cow horns are made of *keratin* (say: KAIR-uh-tin)—that's the same stuff your fingernails are made of! Inside each horn is a bit of bone connected right to the cow's head. And here's the cool part: unlike deer antlers that fall off and grow back, cow horns stay for life and just keep on growing!

ALL THINGS COWS FOR KIDS

Here's a fun fact:

*Horns depend on breed, not gender, so both males and females can have horns! Some types of cattle, like Highland cows and Texas Longhorns, are famous for their dramatic horns. Others are naturally born without them—these are called **polled** cattle.*

Got a little headgear trim!

Back in the wild days, horns helped protect cows from predators. Today, some farmers gently remove horns to keep cows from accidentally injuring each other—or the people caring for them.

EYES: PEEK-A-MOO VISION

Set on the sides of their head, cow eyes give them super wide vision—almost 330 degrees! That means they can see nearly everything around them without turning their head. Pretty handy for spotting friends (*or the yummiest piece of grass*) from all angles.

But watch out—cows have two small blind spots: right behind them and just under their nose. That's

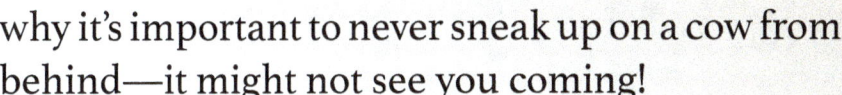

why it's important to never sneak up on a cow from behind—it might not see you coming!

TONGUE: THE GRASS GRABBER

A cow's tongue is long, strong, and a little bit rough—perfect for pulling up big mouthfuls of grass. It can stretch up to 12 inches (30 cm) and works like a scoop, wrapping around grass and pulling it right into their mouths.

It's also covered in tiny bumps that feel kind of like sandpaper—great for gripping food, but not so great for licking your hand! (Though some cows try anyway.)

TEETH: THE GRASS CHOMPERS

It's surprising, but these funky creatures have no upper front teeth! Instead, cows have a tough "dental pad" on the top, and they use their bottom front teeth to press grass against it—snip, snip! It's like built-in scissors.

In the back of their mouths, they have wide, flat molars that grind and mash all that fibrous food into a soft, soupy mush. Cows chew their food twice (*but we will learn all about this in just a second*), so strong teeth are a must!

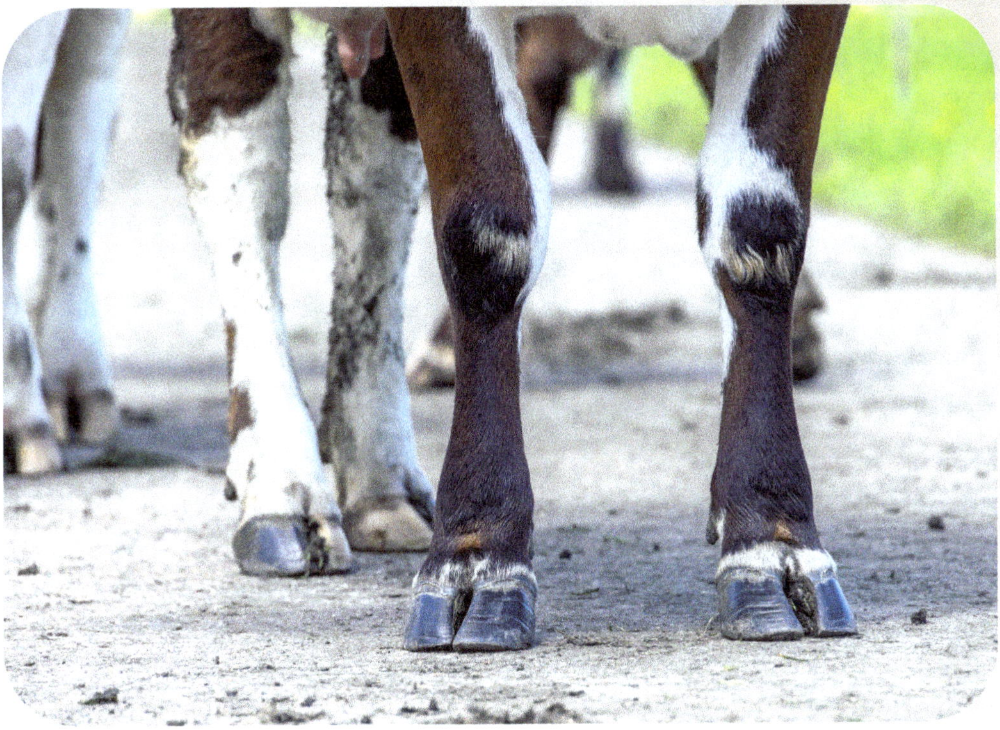

HOOVES: MUD-STOMPING SUPER SHOES

Cows don't wear shoes, but their hooves are just as important. Made of keratin—*yep, the same stuff as their horns and your fingernails*—hooves protect their feet and help them move around.

Each hoof is split in two (*this is called "cloven"*), which helps them balance better, especially on soft, muddy, or uneven ground. And just like toenails, hooves need trimming every now and then to stay comfy and healthy. Cows getting pedicures? *Who would have thought!*

THE TUMMY TEAM: HOW COWS DIGEST LIKE SUPERHEROES

The most amazing thing about a cow isn't on the outside—it's in her belly! While we have just one stomach, cows have *four*, and they all work together like a food factory.

It all starts with the **rumen** (say: ROO-men)—this is the biggest chamber, and it's about the size of a beach ball! It holds up to 50 gallons of food and water (*that's 50 big milk jugs!*). Inside, billions of tiny helpers called microbes get busy breaking down tough grass.

Next is the **reticulum** (say: ruh-TIK-yoo-lum), which acts like a filter. If a cow accidentally swallows something like a rock or nail, this chamber catches it. That's why some farmers call it the "hardware stomach!"

Here comes the weird part: cows bring their food *back up* to chew it again. That half-chewed snack is called **cud**. You've probably seen cows lying in the grass, chewing slowly—they're giving their lunch a second go!

Then the food goes to the **omasum** (say: oh-MAY-sum), which has lots of folds—kind of like a book. It squeezes out water and soaks up nutrients.

Now for the last stop: the **abomasum** (say: ab-oh-MAY-sum), which works like your own tummy, using juices to finish digesting the food and send energy all around the cow's body.

That four-part tummy is a cow's secret superpower, turning plain grass into milk and strength. Now that's one hard-working belly!

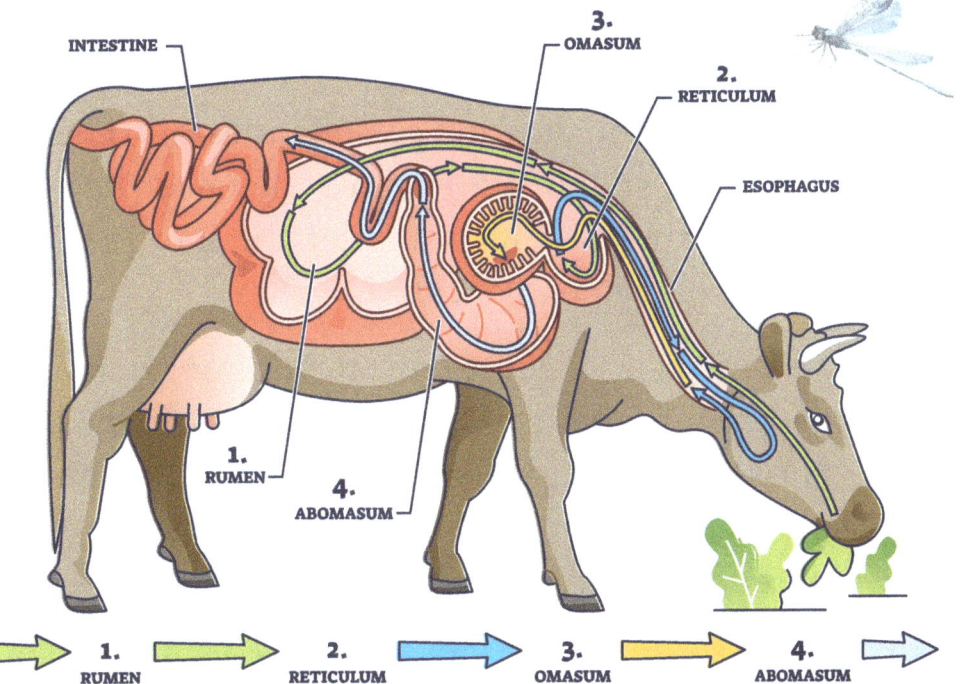

MOO-DS AND MOO-MORIES: GETTING TO KNOW COW PERSONALITIES

Although mostly known for their milk-making skills, cows are much, much more—they are thoughtful, curious animals with personalities all their own. Scientists who study animal behavior have found that cows are much smarter and more sensitive than many people realize.

Cows are social creatures who build strong bonds with others in their herd. They even have best friends! And just like you might feel a bit down if you didn't see your best buddy for a while, cows can feel stressed when separated from theirs.

They also have outstanding memories. Cows can recognize and remember more than 100 other cows—and even human faces—for years. When two cows who know each other meet, they might share a greeting: a soft moo or a friendly head rub.

As you've already learned, cows are curious by nature. They love to check things out—but only once they feel safe. They're calm creatures who like to take their time with anything new. Cows also prefer peace over drama—you won't catch them picking fights! Most of the time, the whole herd moves, grazes, and naps together like one big, relaxed team.

Cows are also pretty clever when it comes to solving problems. They can learn to press buttons with their noses to get food or water, and some even figure out how to open gates (*sneaky smart, right?*). Once a cow solves a puzzle, she often remembers the answer for a long time. On some farms, cows know exactly when it's milking time, and they'll line up all by themselves when they hear the right sounds!

Next time you see a cow in a field, take a moment to really look. Behind those big eyes and slow steps is a clever, curious, and totally surprising animal full of smarts, heart, and a little bit of ***moo*-gic.**

MUNCH & CRUNCH:
WHAT COWS LOVE TO EAT

Now that you know how a cow's tummy works, let's find out what they like to fill it with!

Cows are **herbivores**, which means they only eat plants. But not just any plants—*cows are grass pros*. Their favorite snacks include fresh green grass, yummy clover, tasty alfalfa, and even hay, which is just a fancy name for dried grass. On farms, they sometimes get extra goodies like *corn silage* (chopped-up, slightly fermented corn plants) or special grain mixes to help them grow strong or make more milk.

Here's something you might not know: cows are actually pretty picky eaters! They love soft and leafy plants and will often dig through hay to find the juiciest bits. They use their long, flexible tongues to grab exactly what they want and their super sniffer noses to track down the freshest snacks in the field. So while it might look like they'll chomp away at anything, cows are careful eaters who know exactly what they like!

Farm cows, those raised for milk or meat, often get a balanced diet called *feed*, which might include:

1. Grains like corn for energy;
2. Soybean meal for protein;
3. Vitamins and minerals to stay healthy;
4. Fiber to keep their digestion running smoothly.

What cows eat largely depends on their job: dairy cows need lots of energy to make milk, while beef cattle need more protein to build muscle.

Once a cow has eaten her fill, she can spend hours chewing her cud—that's the second round of munching that helps break down tough plant fibers.

ALL THINGS COWS FOR KIDS

MILK MAGIC: HOW COWS FILL YOUR GLASS

Girl cows are natural milk machines! Once a cow has her first baby calf, her body starts making milk in special parts called *mammary glands*. These connect to her *udder*—that soft, pink bag hanging under her belly.

A cow's udder has four parts, and each one has its own *teat* (that's the bit the milk comes out of). It's like she has four little milk factories running at the same time!

Dairy cows can make **a *lot*** of milk—up to 8 gallons every day. That's more than 100 glasses of milk from just one cow! Imagine the big milk jug in your fridge—if it holds one gallon, a cow can fill eight of those every single day!

Farmers usually milk cows two or three times a day using special machines that gently pump the milk out. A long time ago, they had to milk every cow

by hand—one squeeze at a time! It took forever! Modern milking machines are much faster and gentler nowadays, and they help farmers care for many cows at once.

WHAT DO YOU GET WHEN A COW JUMPS ON A TRAMPOLINE?

Milkshake!

THE MOO-NIVERSE OF COWS:
MEET THE BREEDS

Did you know there are over 800 different breeds of cattle around the world? That's even more than the number of dog breeds! Over thousands of years, farmers have raised each kind for different jobs—some are great at making milk, some are built for beef, and others are tough enough to live in hot deserts or chilly mountains.

Let's meet some of the most amazing cow breeds from around the globe. And we'll start with a real superstar—the one you've probably drawn, spotted in a cartoon, or seen munching in a field!

HOLSTEINS: THE SPOTTED MILK MACHINES

When most people picture a cow, they imagine black and white spots—that's a Holstein! These cows are the most common dairy breed in the world, and for good reason: **they make more milk than any other cow.**

I'm a Holstein—I'm spotted, and I know it!

One Holstein can produce up to **9 gallons (34 liters)** of milk every day—that's about **144 glasses**! In a year, that adds up to more than **28,000 pounds (12,700 kilograms)** of milk. That's heavier than a school bus!

Holsteins are big, too. They stand around 4.5 feet (1.4 meters) tall at the shoulder and can be over 8 feet (2.4 meters) long—about the size of a small car. Most weigh between 1,300 and 1,500 pounds (590–680 kilograms), which is a LOT! Despite their impressive size, Holsteins are known for being gentle and easy to handle.

Most Holsteins have that classic black-and-white look, but some are red and white instead, thanks to a special gene. And just like snowflakes or our own fingerprints, no two spot patterns are the same!

Some Holsteins, like this calf, can have a red and white coat too!

Holsteins originally came from the Netherlands, where farmers began breeding them over 2,000 years ago. Nowadays, you will find them on dairy farms all over the world—from the U.S. and Canada to Japan and South Africa.

With their **friendly nature, calm attitude, and super milk powers**, it's no wonder Holsteins are some of the most loved cows on Earth!

Fun Fact:

One Holstein cow can give over 100 glasses of milk a day. That means if a class of 25 kids drank 1 glass of milk each, one cow could keep them going for four days, with extra to spare for cereal or cookies!

ANGUS ALL-STARS: THE MASTERS OF BEEF

If Holsteins are milk champions, **then consider Angus the #1 beef experts**. These solid-colored cows—usually black, sometimes red—are known for their strength, calm nature, and super tasty meat.

Angus cattle are **naturally polled**, which means they're born without horns. This makes them easier to manage and safer for other cattle and farmers.

They're medium-sized, standing about 4 to 4.5 feet (1.2–1.4 meters) tall and weighing 1,200 to 1,800 pounds (545–820 kilograms). It would take about 10 kids to match the weight of one full-grown Angus cow!

Built tough, born smart—
say hello to the Angus crew!

Their dark coats help them stay warm in chilly weather, which is perfect for their original home: the cold hills of Scotland.

That's where the breed began—in places called Aberdeenshire and Angus (which is how they got their name). Angus cattle were brought to the U.S. in 1873 and quickly became popular for their strength and easy-going personalities.

Fun Fact:

Angus cattle are known for being extra calm and clever. They're quick to learn routines—like when it's time to eat or move fields—and they don't spook easily. That's why farmers say Angus cows are some of the easiest and friendliest to work with on the farm!

HIGHLAND COWS: THE FUZZY FRIENDS OF THE HILLS

With their long, shaggy hair and big, swoopy horns, Highland cows look like they've stepped out of a storybook. These fluffy cows come from the cold, windy hills of Scotland, where the weather can be wet, snowy, and super chilly.

To stay warm, Highlands have two layers of hair. The soft, fuzzy undercoat keeps them toasty, while the longer top layer works like a raincoat. It blocks out the wind, rain, and snow. That's why Highland cows can live outside all year round, even in the middle of winter.

No bad hair days here—just Highland cow style!

Highlands are smaller than some other breeds, standing around 4 feet (1.2 meters) tall and about 6 feet (1.8 meters) long. But don't be fooled by their smaller size—they're tough, smart, and full of personality.

Highland cows can be red, black, white, **or yellow, and both boys and girls grow big, curving horns** that point out and up like fancy headbands.

These cows are **expert foragers.** They can find food on steep hills and rocky places where other cows wouldn't even try to reach.

ALL THINGS COWS FOR KIDS

Fun Fact:

Highland cows **are known for** their sweet and gentle nature. They're especially loved on small farms, and some people even keep them as pets.

TEXAS LONGHORNS: HORNS, HISTORY, AND THE WILD WILD WEST

With their **huge, curving horns** and bold colors, Texas Longhorns are true stars of the American West. Their horns can grow up to **7 feet (2.1 meters) wide, which is even wider than a car!** Both

With horns like these, we had to be called something special!

males and females grow horns, although bulls usually have the biggest ones. Their coats come in all kinds of colors—red, black, white, yellow, and every speckled mix you can imagine. No two Longhorns look the same!

These tough cows are the descendants of Spanish cattle brought to the Americas in the 1500s. Over time, they learned how to survive in the wild—handling heat, drought, and predators all on their own.

After the Civil War, cowboys rounded up wild Longhorns and drove them on long trips to railroads in the north. These famous cattle drives helped shape the stories and legends of the Wild West.

By the early 1900s, Longhorns were nearly gone, but thanks to people who wanted to protect them, these amazing cows are thriving once again—strong, smart, and proud symbols of cowboy country.

Fun Fact:

Texas Longhorns hold the world record for longest horns—one famous bull had horns that reached over 10 feet (3 meters) from tip to tip! That's longer than a car... and almost as wide as a small school bus!

GIR COWS: THE FLOPPY-EARED BEAUTIES OF INDIA

Floppy ears and gentle eyes... meet the Gir Cow!

With their **droopy ears, calm eyes, and gentle** nature, Gir cows are easy to spot—and even easier to love! These beautiful cows come from Gujarat, a hot and dry part of western India.

Gir cows are part of a group called Zebu cattle (or *Bos indicus*). That means they have some cool features made for tropical weather—like a little hump on their back, and a loose flap of skin under their neck called a dewlap. And those big, floppy ears? They're not just cute—they help keep the cow cool by letting out heat!

Most Gir cows are reddish-brown with white spots and light rings around their eyes and nose—like

they're wearing fancy makeup! They're strong and sturdy, growing up to 5 feet tall and 7 feet long.

In India, **Gir cows are treated like part of the family.** During festivals, people dress them up with colorful cloths, flowers, and bells. They even get special treats to show they're loved.

Gir cows also make a special kind of milk called A2, which some people find easier to digest. It's rich, creamy, and perfect for making ghee, a buttery favorite in Indian cooking.

Because they're so calm and good at handling heat, Gir cows are now popular in other hot countries too, like Brazil and Mexico.

ALL THINGS COWS FOR KIDS 51

Fun Fact:

During special holidays, Gir cows are treated like queens! People paint their horns, drape them in colorful fabrics, and hang flower garlands around their necks. Some even get their own snacks and music—now that's a party fit for a cow!

Muscles, horns, and a whole lot of confidence... meet the Toro Bravo!

THE TORO BRAVO: MUSCLE, SPEED, AND SPIRIT

The **Toro Bravo** (say: TOR-oh BRAH-voh) is one of the strongest and fastest cows in the world. These powerful animals are sleek, muscular, and full of energy.

Toro Bravos can grow up to 5 feet tall and 7 feet long. Most have black or dark brown coats and big, curved horns that point forward. They look pretty serious—and they are!

They live on big, open ranches in Spain called ganaderías (say: gah-nah-deh-REE-ahs), where they roam freely in small family groups. The girl bulls, called **vacas bravas**, are very protective mothers. Both bulls and cows use their strength and speed to keep their herd safe from danger.

ALL THINGS COWS FOR KIDS 53

Toro Bravos are still raised for traditional events like bullfighting and the Running of the Bulls. They were chosen for these roles because of their strength, speed, and spirit. But today, more people are looking for ways to celebrate these incredible animals without putting them in danger—through safer events, shows, and conservation efforts.

Bullfighting is becoming less and less popular, and now more festivals are popping up that honor these majestic animals without harming them.

With their bold horns, quick reflexes, and proud style, Toro Bravos are truly one-of-a-kind.

ANIMAL READS

Fun Fact:

A Toro Bravo can run faster than a racehorse at full gallop—up to 35 miles per hour (56 km/h)! With those strong legs and quick turns, these bulls are like the superheroes of the cow world. Don't blink—you might miss them!

No matter the breed... we're all pretty cool!

WHY DID THE COW ASK FOR A TELESCOPE?

She wanted to see the Milky Way!

WHERE IN THE WORLD DO COWS LIVE?

From snowy mountain meadows to tropical grasslands, cows have learned to live just about everywhere—except Antarctica (*even the fluffiest Highland cow would say 'no thanks' to that much ice!*).

Altogether, there are over *1.5 billion* cattle on Earth, nearly one cow for every five people!

Some countries have *huge* cattle populations. India has the most, with more than **300 million**! Many of these cows are considered sacred in the local Hindu culture and are treated with kindness and respect. Brazil is next with about **230 million**, followed by China with around **100 million**, and the United States with about **95 million**.

Let's take a little trip to learn more about the special places cows call home:

In Switzerland, cows spend their summers high up in the Alps, wearing big, loud bells so farmers

can hear them in the mist. When it's time to come down in autumn, they're dressed in flowers and celebrated in cheerful parades called *Alpabzug* (ALP-ab-tsoog) or *Désalpe* (day-ZALP). It's like a cow fashion show!

In India, cows can be found in city streets, calmly walking through traffic. People often offer them food as a sign of respect, and these clever cows have learned to navigate the hustle and bustle. Some of these cows are so used to traffic they've learned to wait for red lights before crossing the street. Smart **mooooves!**

Looking fancy for the big parade!

In Africa, communities like the *Maasai* move with their cattle, walking great distances to find fresh grass after the rains. The cows and their people travel side by side—through sun, rain, and even dust storms. The Maasai know each cow by sight and care for them like family.

In New Zealand, cows graze on some of the greenest pastures in the world, surrounded by stunning mountains. These cows munch grass in fields so green, they look like they came from a storybook! You might've even seen these hills in movies with dragons or wizards.

In Argentina, cattle roam the vast *Pampas* grasslands and are cared for by skilled cowboys known as *gauchos* (say: GOW-chose), who have their own unique traditions and style. They ride fast horses, wear wide-brimmed hats, and use long sticks to guide their cattle across the plains.

Cattle, cowboys, and wide-open skies!

In the Netherlands, where Holstein cows were first bred, some creative farmers have built floating dairy farms. Yes—cows living on platforms that float in the water, right in cities like Rotterdam! These floating farms even have little bridges so cows can enjoy the sunshine outside. Milk from these

In Africa, communities like the *Maasai* move with their cattle, walking great distances to find fresh grass after the rains. The cows and their people travel side by side—through sun, rain, and even dust storms. The Maasai know each cow by sight and care for them like family.

In New Zealand, cows graze on some of the greenest pastures in the world, surrounded by stunning mountains. These cows munch grass in fields so green, they look like they came from a storybook! You might've even seen these hills in movies with dragons or wizards.

In Argentina, cattle roam the vast *Pampas* grasslands and are cared for by skilled cowboys known as *gauchos* (say: GOW-chose), who have their own unique traditions and style. They ride fast horses, wear wide-brimmed hats, and use long sticks to guide their cattle across the plains.

Cattle, cowboys, and wide-open skies!

In the Netherlands, where Holstein cows were first bred, some creative farmers have built floating dairy farms. Yes—cows living on platforms that float in the water, right in cities like Rotterdam! These floating farms even have little bridges so cows can enjoy the sunshine outside. Milk from these

floating farms is sometimes collected by boat instead of truck.

No matter where they live, cows have adapted to all kinds of environments, climates, and cultures. From city streets to mountaintops, cows are at home almost everywhere—and the world wouldn't be the same without them.

WATCH OUT, PREDATORS!

Long ago, wild cattle had to stay alert for danger. Their ancestors, the *aurochs*, were strong animals that used their horns and hooves to fight off predators like wolves, big cats, and bears.

Today's cows usually live safely on farms, but in places like the American West or the Australian outback, cows sometimes still face threats from wild animals like coyotes or wild dogs called dingoes. That's one reason some cattle still have horns and why farmers keep guard dogs with their herds.

Even the calmest cow will kick up a fuss if her calf is in danger. In the wild or on open pastures, cows will surround their calves if they sense trouble. They will stand facing out, ready to defend the little ones.

These hooves? Not to be messed with!

Don't forget, cows can be very big! A full-grown adult can weigh over 1,500 pounds (680 kilograms) and deliver a mighty kick. Enough to convince most predators to look for an easier meal somewhere else!

WHAT SAYS "OOOOOOO..."?

A cow with no lips!

GROWING UP BOVINE:
FROM WOBBLY CALF TO MIGHTY COW

Every cow starts life as a wobbly-legged baby and grows into a big, powerful adult through one amazing journey. Let's follow their life stage by stage and see how they change and grow along the way.

BABY CALVES (BIRTH TO 6 MONTHS)

After about **9 months** of growing inside their mother (*just like humans!*), a baby calf is born. Most arrive front legs and head first, like they're diving into the world!

Calves weigh 60 to 100 pounds (27 to 45 kilograms) when they're born—about the same size as a large dog. Their coats are soft and fuzzy, and the color can even change as they grow. Within just **an hour**, most calves are already standing on their own. That's super important, especially for wild calves that **need** to keep up with the herd right away.

The very first thing they drink is a special kind of milk called **colostrum**. It's full of nutrients and antibodies that help protect them from getting sick. For the first few months, calves drink milk and begin learning how to eat solids like hay and grain.

They grow quickly—up to 2 pounds a day! At first, only one part of their four-chambered stomach works (*the abomasum—the one similar to ours*). As they continue to nibble more solid food, the rumen (*the first biggest chamber*) begins to grow and get stronger.

ALL THINGS COWS FOR KIDS 67

By around **8 weeks**, they're chewing a little cud and eating more solids. By **6 months**, most calves are fully **weaned** (*this means they don't drink their mom's milk anymore*) and getting all their nutrients from grass, hay, or feed—just like the grown-up cows.

GROWING UP (6 MONTHS TO 2 YEARS)

After calves stop drinking milk, they enter their "teenager" stage—a time when they do a lot of growing and learning!

Young girl cows are called **heifers**, and young boys are called **bullocks**. These growing cows can gain up to **2.5 pounds (1.1 kilograms)** every day!

By now, teenage cows start looking more like adults. Beef breeds get strong and muscular, while dairy breeds stay leaner and lighter on their feet. But they're not just growing—they're also learning how to be part of the herd. This is when cows figure out who's in charge, how to make friends, and how to communicate with each other using body language, gentle nudges, and—of course—moos.

Cattle are naturally curious and still playful at this age. Young males sometimes play-fight, while others chase, explore, and test boundaries—just like human teens!

LIFE AS A COW (ADULTHOOD AND BEYOND)

By the time cows turn two years old, they've become adults. Some keep growing a little more until they're about four, but they've mostly reached their full size by now. As adults, they settle into calm, cozy routines, spending their days grazing, resting, and socializing with their friends. Dairy cows may get milked a few times a day, while beef cattle enjoy long, lazy days out in the pasture. With good care, cows can live a long time. Most farm cows live **4 to 6 years**, but those in sanctuaries or as pets can live to be **15 to 25 years** old. The oldest cow ever recorded made it to 48 years!

As cows get older, their teeth wear down and their joints get a little stiff, but they don't lose their gentle nature. They remember their favorite friends—*both cow and human*—and enjoy a peaceful life with the herd.

YOU ARE LEGEN-DAIRY!

MIND-BLOWING MOOING FACTS!

Now that you know all about these incredible animals, get ready for some seriously surprising cow facts that just might make you say… *holy cow!*

You've learned a ton about cows—but these final moo-velous facts might just blow your barn boots off.

THE GREAT COW COMPASS

When cows rest or graze, they tend to face **north or south**—as if they're using Earth's magnetic field! Scientists spotted this pattern using satellite images, but no one knows why they do it. Built-in GPS, maybe?

MUSICAL MOO-DS

Cows love music! Studies show they relax and even make **more milk** when listening to slow tunes like soft jazz or classical music. Some dairy farms play calming songs in the barn every day.

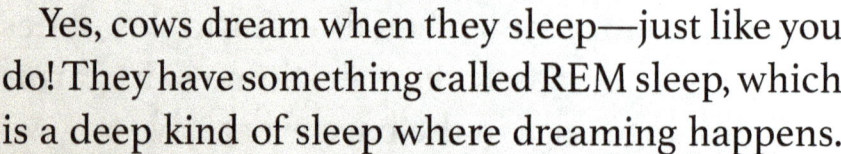

Got a good beat? I'll moo along!

MOO-MORIES THAT LAST

Cows have great memories. They can recognize the **faces of over 100 other cows**—and remember people, too! Some even recall favorite spots in a pasture **years** after visiting them.

COWS THAT DREAM

Yes, cows dream when they sleep—just like you do! They have something called REM sleep, which is a deep kind of sleep where dreaming happens.

Farmers have seen cows twitch their legs, wiggle their ears, or even let out a little "moo" while they snooze. What do you think they dream about? Yummy grass? Fresh clover? Who knows!

SAY WHAT, COW?

Cows don't moo the same way every time. They have **different calls** for hunger, danger, or finding their calf—and mothers and babies can pick out each other's voice in a crowd. It's their own secret cow language.

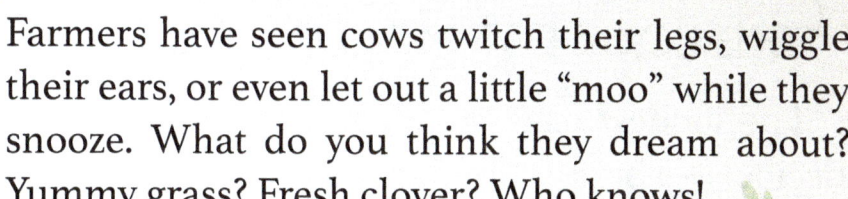

THE LOUDEST MOO ON RECORD

The loudest cow "moo" ever recorded hit 125 decibels—about as loud as a rock concert! That's one serious sound system for a barnyard animal.

SUPER SOFT NOSES

Ever touched a cow's nose? It's one of the **softest things you'll ever feel**—warm, velvety, and always a little damp. Cows use their sensitive noses to explore, sniff, and even nuzzle their friends!

CONGRATULATIONS—
YOU'RE NOW A CERTIFIED CATTLE WHISPERER!

You did it! You've just moo-ved through an incredible journey into the world of cows. From their four-part super stomachs to their gentle personalities, from curious calves to wise adults, you now know what makes these animals truly amazing.

The next time you spot cows grazing in a field, you'll see so much more than just "farm animals." You'll know about their best friends, their memory superpowers, and their one-of-a-kind "moo" voices. You'll spot the difference between dairy and beef breeds—and you might even notice if they're standing in a north-south line!

There's still so much more to explore in the world of farm animals, and we hope this is just the beginning. Maybe you'll visit a local dairy or cattle ranch and meet some cows in person. And be sure to share your new cow knowledge—you're now the go-to expert in your family!

Thanks for joining us on this moo-velous adventure. You're officially a cow expert—**and we're so <u>udderly</u> proud of you!**

Thanks a MOOO-llion!

WHAT WOULD YOU GET IF YOU CROSS AN ANGRY SHEEP AND A GRUMPY COW?

An animal that's totally in a BAAAAAd MOOOOOd!

THANK YOU!

Thank you for reading this book and for allowing us to share our love for cows with you!

If you've enjoyed this book, please let us know by leaving a rating and a brief review wherever you made your purchase! This helps us spread the word to other readers!

Thank you for your time, and have an awesome day!

For more information, please visit:
www.animalreads.com

© Copyright 2025—All rights reserved Admore Publishing

ISBN: 978-3-96772-194-2

ISBN: 978-3-96772-195-9

ISBN: 978-3-96772-196-6

Animal Reads at www.animalreads.com

The content contained within this book may not be reproduced, duplicated or transmitted without direct written permission from the author or the publisher.

Under no circumstances will any blame or legal responsibility be held against the publisher, or author, for any damages, reparation, or monetary loss due to the information contained within this book. Either directly or indirectly.

Published by Admore Publishing: Gotenstraße, Berlin, Germany

www.admorepublishing.com

www.ingramcontent.com/pod-product-compliance
Lightning Source LLC
LaVergne TN
LVHW020140080526
838202LV00048B/3980